ABUNDANCE WHISPERS

PATHWAY TO PROSPERITY

CHITRA IYENGAR

Copyright © Chitra Iyengar
All Rights Reserved.

ISBN 978-1-68563-185-7

This book has been published with all efforts taken to make the material error-free after the consent of the author. However, the author and the publisher do not assume and hereby disclaim any liability to any party for any loss, damage, or disruption caused by errors or omissions, whether such errors or omissions result from negligence, accident, or any other cause.

While every effort has been made to avoid any mistake or omission, this publication is being sold on the condition and understanding that neither the author nor the publishers or printers would be liable in any manner to any person by reason of any mistake or omission in this publication or for any action taken or omitted to be taken or advice rendered or accepted on the basis of this work. For any defect in printing or binding the publishers will be liable only to replace the defective copy by another copy of this work then available.

Contents

Acknowledgements v

1. Chapter 1   1
2. Chapter 2   6
3. Chapter 3   13
4. Chapter 4   16
5. Chapter 5   20
6. Chapter 6   31
7. Chapter 7   35
8. Chapter 8   38
9. Chapter 9   45

COMMANDMENTS

Acknowledgements

Thank you ....

My dear son Haridya Iyengar, for his belief in me, his unstinting support and encouragement.

My family- a constant source of motivation and encouragement in my life.

Zaya, for patiently creating the beautiful Cover page for my book.

Mr. Irfan Noorani, for his support and hand-holding.

Mrs. Neeta Hotkar for her technical help.

God Bless Everybody.

CHAPTER ONE

ABUNDANCE WHISPERS
Pathway to prosperity
Have faith in your journey,
Everything had to happen exactly as it did,
To get you where you're going Next.
~ Mandy Hale

Zach felt something cold and wet drop into his palm. Shivers went up his arms. You never know what sort of creatures are crawling in these chill, dark mountain regions. Then he noticed that it was already quite bright outside. The early morning sun had risen in a beautiful orange yellow hue, with a few grey clouds lingering, reluctant to leave the sky. He wondered why his vision was blurred; perhaps he was still drowsy? Then he realized that the wetness was on his face. Surprised, he realized that tears were streaming down his face. He slowly looked at his hand. A wet tissue lay there. He wiped his face and felt better.

How long had he been crying? He could not believe he had lost everything again, but this time it seemed worse. This was his last chance to bring some sanity into his life. If this venture did not work out, he might as well jump off the Everest. This quest seemed like his last chance in life. He could not think of anything else.

Why? Why was this happening to him? Where had he gone wrong? Why do things keep going wrong with him?

Was he jinxed? 'Gosh', he thought, 'what am I thinking. Jinxed, honestly?'. Meticulous, to the T, he always went out of his way to do his best. He was always there for his friends and family. He was a handsome man in his mid-40s. He had been rich till a few months ago. WHY WAS IT ALWAYS HIM?? He was fed up with the yo yo life was dolling out to him.

He felt the same dampness in his palm again and saw the lady next to him looking discreetly into her bag. He had not realized that tears had been streaming down his face again. He had not cried like this ever in his life, not even when his father forcibly dragged him to the boarding school at the age of 8; not even when he had found his darling wife cozy with his close friend, when he had returned from a life-threatening stint with the rebels in the amazon forests.

He wiped his face with the wet tissue so kindly supplied by his neighbor next seat and said "thank you". She turned and smiled at him. Wow. It was as if all the bulbs in the bus had been switched on. He had never seen a more powerful smile. It started with her lips and travelled slowly to her heavy-lidded eyes. He was not poetic by any stretch of imagination, but the thought- doe eyes came to his mind immediately. He kept gazing into its depth, until she said softly-"Hello, I am Yamini" he responded- " Hi. I am Zachery" seeing the expression on her face, he said-"I know it's a mouthful. You can call me Zach. Most people do".

He looked at Yamini again- a pretty and charming face with deep laughter lines running down a nose which was a little big for her face. He couldn't stop smiling at the thought. She had strong bow shaped lips and smooth unlined face. "make-up" the photographer in him thought. But no, the moisture on her face was real. She really had amazing pink toned skin. He could not gauge her age- she seemed to be in her 40s, No - 30s? Very confusing. She had one of those ageless looks. He saw her squirming uncomfortably under his intense gaze and started chuckling-"Sorry. Please don't get me wrong. I am a freelance photographer and journalist. Professional hazard. I start observing people minutely. Many get me wrong; specially the ladies." He said ruefully. She relaxed and started laughing-" I thought probably there was a toad sitting on my nose" she said. He pictured a little frog sitting on the tip of her nose and started laughing with her.

She continued- "I noticed the bold Z on your backpack and was wondering if it was your initials, but I wasn't sure". she was much more observant than him, he thought. She had observed his custom-made back-pack and camera kit with his initials embossed. Of course, they were worth noticing. They were also reminders from his millionaire days. Tears were about to burst from his eyes. He controlled them consciously and looked around the bus. It was a luxurious Volvo, quite comfortable too, except that his long legs would not really fit into the space. Despite having the seat in the 1st row, his 6ft 6 inches frame was really crammed in the space. Even on flights he had to always request for seats with extra leg space, and this was India where people were comparatively petite. Yamini had her legs folded under her and it still looked like 2 of her could fit into her seat.

Given the state of his mind, he had not noticed anyone or anything in the bus. The lighting had also been dim when he boarded it last night at Delhi. The bus was at least 60-70% full and the passengers were dozing in their seats or just waking up. Soft chatter could be heard as passengers woke up. Suddenly the bus swerved to the side of the road and stopped, bouncing softly. The bus attendant announced that everyone could get down for some tea and snacks. Zack eagerly jumped up and hit his head on the luggage rack above. Damn!!...why do they make these buses for pygmies??

Yamini unfurled her legs gracefully and stood up. She was much shorter than he thought, barely reaching above his elbows. He impatiently waited for her to move, which she quickly did when she saw him uncomfortably stooped under the luggage rack. With a quick thank you, he gratefully jumped out of the bus.

The cold mountain air hit him and he started shivering. He was wearing cutout T-shirt to combat the Delhi heat, and his jackets were packed into the suitcase stashed into the belly of the bus. He felt something being thrust into his hand, but this time not cold and wet but warm and soft. His Angel Yamini, of course. The shawl barely covered his shoulders, but he did feel much better. They looked at each other and burst out laughing. He couldn't remember when he had laughed so freely the last time. He drank the thick sweet hot tea and felt energy flow into him. He must have had atleast 3 cups until he was satisfied. People around were shocked, and then started clapping when they heard him conversing fluently in Hindi. He looked really embarrassed. He was pretty good with languages and having gone around the globe at-least 4-5 times, had picked up many languages and could speak at-least 9 languages fluently, Hindi being one of them.

Boarding the bus once again, they started on their journey. Soon Yamini's head started nodding. After some time, it dropped on his shoulders. He adjusted himself to make it more comfortable for her. Afterall, he thought, with a looped grin, this was the least he could do for her after having nearly exhausted her wet wipes.

CHITRA IYENGAR

CHAPTER TWO

Life shrinks or expands in proportion to one's Courage
~Anais Nin

Suddenly lightning streaked across the sky and clouds started thundering. The suddenness of the weather change was shocking and scary too. It started pouring heavily. Zack didn't remember seeing such a downpour since he had left the Amazon Rain forests. Especially when he was on the road. Being crazily addicted to driving, he could understand the challenge the driver was facing, holding the bus to the road. Water steadily started rising on the road and visibility was zero due to the heavy downpour. The bus was literally crawling and that too, uphill. The AC was switched off to give the bus additional power to push against the gushing water and climb up. The skies had darkened and the dim lights in the bus were switched on. Everybody was tensed and a few were praying fervently. A small baby started wailing. The crescendo started increasing till it was howling loudly. The mother, a young girl, embarrassingly started feeding her milk to the baby, to calm it down. Nobody noticed, just so thankful that the crying had stopped. Zack realized that in all the cacophony, his tears had stopped. He had not thought about his problems for over an hour. He wasn't sure if his worries were better or this scary light and sound show that the skies were putting up.

Suddenly the bus turned right and kept turning right and right. It crashed into the thin barricade on the edge of the road and started bumping and plunging down the hill. People started screaming, jostling against each other. Luggage from the rack above was falling all over the bus.

Just as suddenly, the bus stopped moving. Everybody held their breath, waiting for the next move, too scared to even turn their heads, lest the bus starts hurtling again. After what seemed an eternity Zack slowly looked out of the window. Sitting right behind the driver, he could see that the bus had wedged itself against a tree, but for how long?

Icy wind blew into the bus, adding to their shivers. Zach looked behind and saw that the glass at the back of the bus had broken badly and a branch was protruding into the bus. He turned slowly in his seat, then gradually got up from his seat. The bus held on. With his heart thundering, he crossed Yamini and walked to the back of the bus. Everybody was watching him with bated breath. He tested the part of the branch inside the bus. It was flimsy, but the portion outside the bus seemed strong. Whether it was strong enough to hold his massive weight was another story, but no time to ponder right now. He gently but firmly started breaking the shattered glass to make a bigger hole, big enough for him to crawl through. He was risking his life and that of everyone in the bus. Nobody knew how much shaking the bus could take, but the risk had to be taken. He held on to the branch and maneuvered himself out of the bus through the hole. As soon as he put his weight on the branch, it started cracking. Not knowing how far the ground was, he let go of the branch which sprung back into the bus with a whack. His uptown latest mountain shoes supported his weight and helped him stand on his feet.

He saw a small lad of about 14-15 years of age climbing out of the bus- onto the branch. When the boy had cleared the bus, Zack held his leg and helped him to the ground. The bus attendant tried his luck next. But the branch broke as he was crawling out of the bus and he ended up with a deep gash on his thigh. He literally rolled out of the bus screaming in pain, but Zach and the boy managed to catch him and lay him on the ground a little away from the bus. Icy cold rain was belting upon them, stinging their face and skin. It was also washing the attendant's wounds and hopefully, numbing his pain.

The bus was totally supported by the tree it had crashed into, but for how long?! Zack explained his plan to the lad and both started rolling boulders to place them in front of the bus tires. It was a slow and painful process, but both of them managed to place boulders in front of the rear tires. They dare not meddle with the front tires which were already in a precarious position. Zack asked the passenger peeping from the nearby window, watching all the proceedings, to open the bus door which was locked from inside. The man carefully moved from his seat and did as he was told, but the door was stuck. It had to be opened with a little pressure and crazy shaking of the bus, which again caused everybody's BP to shoot up and some more screams. Zack asked everybody to leave their luggage and come out of the bus slowly, one by one.

He noticed little orange clothed figures running from the road above towards the bus with stacks of logs on their shoulder. He was wondering how the hell they were going to light a fire in the pouring rain and who the hell were they? As they came closer, he saw that they seemed to be little boys from the Buddhist monastery uphill. They were carrying sturdy sticks which they started handing over to the passengers who were getting out of the bus. It was to help them climb up the hill, especially in the slippery wet soil which was also getting washed away in the torrent.

The bus driver was in severe shock and not moving from his seat, despite everybody calling out to him. Zach cautiously entered the bus and tried to speak to the driver to come out of his seat, but nothing was entering the driver's brains. He sat there like a statue, both his hand holding the steering wheel tightly. Zach opened the driver's fingers one by one and released his arms. He pulled him bodily out of the seat. The bus started shaking violently. He quickly passed him over to helping hands and rushed to his seat to pull out his back pack and camera kit. The bus was now dancing crazily and people were screaming at him to jump out immediately.

He threw his back pack out and jumped out of the bus, holding on to his camera kit tightly. The bus started its crazy dance again, but surprisingly stood its ground. Yamini looked at him accusingly and said "you told all of us to leave all our bags in the bus, and now you go and bring both your bags. Not fair". Zach responded sheepishly- "Sorry. But how could I leave my back pack. They hold all my worldly possessions- $1670 and Rs.2340/-. My camera is my passion, my love and also my bread and butter. I would rather die than be without them". She looked at him incredulously-"What rubbish!! Don't you realize how rich you are? You have saved all our lives". And walked away. Zack didn't know whether to laugh or cry. HE, and rich? What a joke.

The passengers were slowly climbing uphill, with the help of the stick. The little monks were also helping by carrying some bags or holding some people. Some people were supporting the bus attendant and helping him limp uphill while some were helping the driver, who was gradually coming out of his shock, with the cold rains hitting him. He was weeping uncontrollably. How funny. The rains had stopped Zack from crying and was making the driver cry. With a shake of his head, Zach gave a final look at the bus, slung his back pack on his shoulder and started trekking up.

The rains were pouring like the heavens was emptying itself. After what seemed an eternity, all the passengers were standing on the road in knee deep water. Two police men and afew Buddhist monks were also waiting for them there. Zack dragged himself up the last few steps, weary from his adventures.

Everybody started clapping and thanking him; One man even called him Superman while another came forward to touch him and shake his hands. Many had tears while thanking him. Zack couldn't understand what extraordinary feat he had accomplished. Anybody in his place would have done the same. While One lady said he was God sent, another called him Bhagwan- God, for saving all their lives.

Yamini came up to him, laid her hands on his arms and said "You are very brave. I know you were surprised when I earlier said that you were very rich. People think only the money in their wallet is their wealth. But Zack, tell me. What use would even a million dollars have been if all of us had crashed into the valley today and died. Do you realize that the wealth of your bravery has saved all of us? Like a soldier, you put others' safety before your own, risked your life for all of us." Zack was feeling really embarrassed now and told her that anyone in his place would have done the same. She quietly said-"did they?" Zack commented-" that's what surprised me. There were so many people sitting in the bus. They were all praying and waiting for God to come down and help them".

Yamini shook her head-"It's not just about being brave or courageous". When she saw Zack's confused look, she said "yes. There is a vast difference between being brave and being courageous. You were brave. The other passengers were courageous. If everybody had jumped up to show their bravery, the bus would not have withstood it and all of us would have been down, in the valley. Do you know how difficult it is to sit and wait? - wait for the right time, the right thing; especially in such situations- not even knowing if you will be alive to see the right thing happen".

She continued- "As I was saying, it is very important to be brave and courageous, but there's something more important- being able to take the right decision and action at the right time. Many people get paralyzed with fear and cannot think or move. Look at our bus driver. He lost control of his mind and the bus. He is still in its clutches. I will not call the other passengers cowards, but none of them could think of a solution at that moment. Even if they could, they were waiting to see who would take the first step".

"All of us are born brave. Have you ever seen a child who is scared from the day it is born? No. fear is an acquired emotion. If you throw a baby into the water, it begins to flail its arms and legs to swim. But if you keep telling him not to go near the water because he might drown, he will develop a fear of water which will handicap him for life.

Of course, courage and bravery can also be learnt. Parents and teachers can motivate their children. And circumstances also make people brave. We have so many instances where ordinary people do extraordinary feats under dire circumstances. Look at our soldiers. They are ordinary people who learn to even sacrifice their life voluntarily". Zack should know. He had served his stint in Afghanistan.

Listening to Yamini talking hypnotically about such interesting aspects of the mind, Zack did not realize that they had reached the place from where their roller-coaster ride had begun.

CHAPTER THREE

Quiet the mind and the soul will speak
~ Ma Jaya Bhagavati

The monastery was less than a mile away- one kilometre to be precise, and fortunately downhill. Zack doubted if any of them had the strength to take one step uphill. All of them were mentally and physically wacked out. But it was a treacherous path. Even though the ferocity of the rain had reduced, it was still pouring steadily. The stones had loosened dangerously and the mud had turned to slush. One wrong step could send them hurtling down. It was getting darker. Everybody was hungry and thirsty and weary to the bones. But they couldn't stop to rest. Then nobody would be in a position to stand up again. All of them started making their way towards the monastery carefully, sometimes holding each other, sometimes the stick, sometimes the boulders. All their eyes were on the white monastery. It was beckoning them like a light house. As they got closer to it, it seemed to go farther away. They were now walking through a village. It seemed to have around 60-70 houses, some a little stronger than others, but all of them definitely rickety. Walking and crawling through the snaking path, everybody literally fell into the monastery foyer and lay there unmoving, each and every one of them, including the little monks who had bravely come to their rescue and the 2 policemen and the older monks and village folks who helped bring down the injured attendant, the shell-shocked driver and 2 ladies who were old and too frail to walk all the way. How long they lay there on the cold floor, listening to the sound of the rain, nobody knew.

Somewhere down the line, Zack must have dosed off. The wonderful smell of spices floating in the air woke him up. He realized that he was starving. He forced himself up and saw that many were still lying on the ice-cold floor while some were sitting leaning against the wall. Even the wet clothes and cold wind could not move them. But the boys from the monastery were not to be seen anywhere. Soon they came out carrying stacks of bowls. They had washed and changed their clothes and cuddled into long warm woollen Angarkha, an extremely warm double-breasted long robe. They were followed by 3 men carrying a huge cauldron of piping hot food. Next came loaves of bread which were all placed on a cemented table in the centre of the foyer. All the people were requested to come and pick up their food. people tried to stand up and started staggering and collapsed to the floor again. The senior monk told all of them to stay where they were and gave some instructions in the local language. A bright smile lit up the faces of people around Zack. The big and little monks started pouring the Thupka, - spiced soupy noodles and bringing it to the people. The boys got slices of bread and started serving everyone. Dipping slices of bread into the soup and slurping the noodles, everyone got busy. There was pin-drop silence, except for the gulping and slurping. Even though the monks were as tired as everybody else, none of them was having their dinner, including the little ones. They stood silently, waiting to see if the others needed anything. Slowly life seemed to seep into everyone on the floor as food entered their body. They started standing up one by one.

Each one was handed a woollen Angarkha to change into and told to go into the inner dormitory to sleep. The dormitory had numerous neatly arranged bunk beds. Everyone started plonking themselves onto a bed. Zack knew that even four beds put together couldn't fit him. Luckily, he had some clothes in his water-proof backpack, else he would have been only half-clothed. He requested a blanket and some pillows. Immediately the boys rolled out a huge soft carpet on the floor and spread a white sheet over it. Then they placed a flat hard pillow on it and 2 woollen blankets. His bed was ready. He literally felt like Gulliver among the Lilliput.

Others were softly snoring. Some were groaning in pain. Zack was the only one tossing and turning. He couldn't sleep. What if...what if he couldn't submit his interview in time to the sponsors. He did not even have enough money to buy his return ticket. He had come with a one-way ticket and 2 months visa. He had so much to do, and then these rains. He knew what havoc such rains could cause, especially in the mountains. Communication and transportation could close down for days, or even weeks on end, depending on the rains, especially during the monsoons.

CHAPTER FOUR

*Meditation is not a way of making your mind Quiet.
It's a way of entering into the Quiet that is already there
Buried under the 50,000 thoughts the average person
thinks every day.*
~ Deepak Chopra

Somewhere along the way his tiredness must have caught up with him. He woke up to the sound of feet pitter pattering around his 'bed'. He pulled his blanket over his head, but couldn't cut out the noises. He peeped through his blanket and saw the others on the bunk bed happily snoring away. Just his bad luck. His bed was right in front of the door and anybody wanting to go to the washroom or kitchen or anywhere out of the room had to pass by him. Damn. He knew he wouldn't be allowed to sleep in peace any longer. He threw his blankets and sat up. Looking at his diamond studded Rolex, he realized it was barely 6 AM. He must have dosed off for barely 3 hours. It was still dark outside. The rains were not letting up. He folded his blankets, rolled the carpet and after keeping them in the assigned corner, went out into the chilling sit-out. He heard a soft humming and quickly turned his head. Against the wall sat alone figure, folded legs and arms stretched out against the knees, forefinger and thumb linked into a circle – the Chinna mudra. Who else? - but his Angel Yamini! With a crooked smile he stood watching her. What he had thought as humming was actually her chanting the

"Ommm". She continued to chant Om at regular intervals, a soft smile on her lips, oblivious to the chill wind raging around. Gradually her chanting stopped and she sat in perfect stillness, breathing deeply.

She looked so calm, so peaceful, so charming. Peace seemed to radiate from her, calming his frayed nerves. How lucky she was. She didn't seem to have any problems in her life. The torrential rains and being stranded here seemed to make no difference to her. She looked like an Empress, sitting on her throne in her palace. He wished he felt at least a fraction of that calm. Actually, even at the peak of his career, when he was a multi-millionaire and all the ladies used to clutter around him, he had never felt calm or satisfied. There was always a vacuum, a sense of incompleteness. A bleak, faraway look came on his face.

He did not realize that Yamini had opened her eyes and was looking at him with concern. He looked so sad, so weary, as if he was fed up with life. Just as she was about to call out to him, he noticed her. "What is the matter? If you like, you can share with me. Perhaps I could help, maybe not. But I promise you, you will feel better". Zack badly wanted to talk to someone, pour his heart out, all his agony. But years of conditioning stopped him. He had never confided even to his mom, though she was the best. Yamini was after-all a stranger. Apart from her name, he did not know anything about her. Yamini smiled and said " Good morning Zackery Rodriguez. What's troubling you so much that you start weeping at the drop of a hat?" Zack was shocked. "How do you know who I am?"

"There are many who know and follow you Zack, even in India".

"So, why did you look surprised when I mentioned my name?"

Yamini laughed softly- "when I saw you, I wasn't sure. I couldn't believe that I was actually seeing the famous Zachery McInac, sitting next to him in an ordinary bus travelling into the mountains. I wasn't surprised; I was stunned. In fact, I am a big fan of yours. I keep waiting for your articles to be published. In fact, your article about the life and activities of the Cambodian rebels was brilliant. You did a sting operation on them by becoming one of them. And the one with the Tiger militants of Sri Lanka, and your 6 months stint in Antarctica. What about the one on the bio-degeneration of the Amazon Rain Forest. Oh my God. Your photographs are so real, it pierces the heart. When I read your articles, I feel I am actually there with you. And.....which sting operation are you planning in this part of the world now?, or is it a secret?"

"Hold on, hold on" Zach laughed. He suddenly realized that he was laughing a lot since he had met her, more than he had in the past few months. "I am flattered that you know so much about me. And.... As the bus we were travelling was going to Dharamshala, obviously, so was I. No secret mission. I was going there, actually to interview His Holiness, the Dalai Lama. The appointment was for today- 4.30 PM" he said, with a big sigh.

"I understand" Yamini said. "Just trust His Holiness. He will take care of you. He knows the past, present and future. If you are stuck here, I know that there's something good in it for you."

"I don't know what you are talking about" Zach growled, rubbing the back of his neck, irritated by such irrational gibberish. "I just know that if I don't send the interview and photos to the channel by tomorrow morning, I will lose everything I have and more. Apart from the money, my reputation is at stake here".

"Come, sit here" she said, patting a place besides her . "I will show you how to get clarity in such situations". Zack sat down beside her and tried to fold his legs. But his tight jeans was not conducive to the gyrations. Yamini suggested that he lean back against the wall, back erect and stretch his legs in front of him,- which he gratefully did.

Yamini then said "Zack, close your eyes and listen to all the sounds around you and describe them to me". Zack started listening intently and telling her all that he could hear- people talking to each other, a boy singing off tune, clacking of utensils, the sound of temple bell [?], a crow cawing somewhere, a mother calling out to her child and the child replying.....his own heavy breathing.......

Yamini asked –"Zack, do these sounds disturb you?" "No, Not really," he said. "Good," she said. "Now just accept all the sounds in the background and only listen to your breathing. Let your thoughts come and go. Don't stop or control them. But keep listening to your breathing, consciously, as long as you can. Open your eyes whenever you feel you want to".

When he opened his eyes, Yamini was nowhere to be seen. Zach looked at his watch. He had sat there with his eyes closed for exactly 12 minutes and 37 seconds, but it felt like he was waking up refreshed after 6-8 hours of deep sleep. His eyes felt cool and he was feeling much calmer.

CHAPTER FIVE

*Do not take life too seriously,
You will never get out of it Alive
~ Elbert Hubbard*

The fragrance of warm bread wafted throughout the monastery, making Zack realize how ravenous he was. Soon people streamed into the foyer and huge stakes of "Balep" the Tibetan bread of the monasteries was brought to the cement table. A clean white cloth was spread on it and the bread was stacked on it. Large bowls of mountain honey were also brought to the table. Everybody picked up a plate and took their bread and honey and found their place to sit and eat. Even though the rains had eased to a drizzle, there was tension on everybody's face. Zack was relieved that he wasn't the only one in stress.

After breakfast, some people set out to rescue the bus and bring the luggage. Zack stuffed his backpack under a bunk bed, tied its straps securely to its leg, then picked up his camera and went out with them. Each one was handed a plastic raincoat, which of course did not fit Zack. So, he brushed it aside and walked out into the drizzle. He had his own raincoat, but it was lying in his suitcase, safe in the belly of the bus. Each of them picked up a stick, some ropes and started their trek. He tried talking to the other guys, but nobody was in a mood for small talk. They were all single-mindedly on a mission. Quietly, Zack opened his camera and started recording the trek, water gushing around their feet and the mountains around.

They reached the bus and ropes were weaved through the rods and the grills of the bus. The ropes were secured to the nearby trees around the bus securely. Hopefully, the bus would withstand the heavy rains and wind now, and stay put until some solid help arrived to pull it up. The bus driver then opened the belly of the bus and suitcases were lugged out. Men tied two to three suitcases with the rope, lugged it around their shoulders like a backpack and started walking back to the monastery, one by one. Zack tried to help, but he was brushed aside. Even his suitcase was picked up by one of the men. They returned to the monastery in a couple of hours, the whole proceedings faithfully recorded by Zack. When the kids and the little monks saw his camera, they also wanted to be photographed. So, he started shooting around the monastery, including everyone there. He looked around for Yamini. He definitely wanted more than a few pics of her in his album. But she was not to be seen anywhere. On enquiry, he was told that she had gone into the village before breakfast to meet a friend. He felt cheated that she had not told him that she had a friend here or about her plans. But WHY??

Fragrant "Tingmo" bread, was being steamed. The soft dough was kneaded laboriously in large bowls. Then they were divided into small round pieces rolled flat, then cut into long strips, stacked on each other and twisted and twirled to give it a flowery pattern Then these rolls were put on a greased plate and steamed. These steamed rolls were served with a gravy made of diced onion, chopped chillies, garlic and coriander leaves, tossed in olive oil. The whole process of making the flower-shaped bread was so amazing, Zack couldn't help filming it. He thought that perhaps he should become a food blog photographer now. He was sure to lose all his present contracts, anyway. With a sigh, he switched off his camera, put it on charge, sat down beside it and closed his eyes. Gradually, he started automatically observing and absorbing all the sounds around him. After some time, he could hear only his breathing. His stomach was rising and falling rhythmically and he was feeling joy bubbling in him with every breath, for no reason at all. He was feeling so peaceful, he never wanted to open his eyes. A soft smile spread on his face and slowly spread to his closed eyes. Immediately Yamini's smiling face flashed into his memory. His smile widened and he felt happier. He started chuckling at himself, softly. Slowly, he started laughing softly and gradually his laughter grew in volume until he was laughing loudly, with his eyes still closed. So, he couldn't see the other people looking at him strangely and smiling. Gradually, they also started chuckling softly. The kids were pointing at Zack and laughing loudly. Gradually the whole monastery was laughing loudly, not at anyone, just laughing. Tears were streaming down many cheeks. It was as if the floodgates had opened. Everybody had been so stressed out. Zack had heard of laughter therapy, but always thought it was for idiots. How could anyone laugh without reason?? Now he knew. He not only knew that you could laugh without reason, but he also knew that it was spontaneous, and it was also a release, it was happy- a calm happiness he had never felt in his life ever before, and especially now when he had nothing to feel happy about.

Yamini was standing at the doorway, a big grin on her face. Her eyes were moist. Zack instinctively knew that she had entered the dormitory. He opened his eyes and looked straight at her. She was also looking straight at him and smiled at him affectionately. Besides her stood a handsome man of around Zack's age, and almost as tall. He must have been around 6ft 2 inches, lean, fair, and had a neatly trimmed VanDyke beard. Both walked towards Zack. Yamini introduced him to Zack as Dr. Rizwan Saleh, her childhood friend; and went on to say that they had been classmates and friends from the age of 4. After 12th std, she had continued to do her Bachelors and later masters in Psychology, while he joined the medical college to become a doctor. Later he had studied further to become an Orthopedic surgeon. After working in AIMMS in Delhi for a few years, he had found his calling in serving the people in remote localities on the mountains.

Zack asked curiously- "why the mountains. You could serve people anywhere". To which Dr. Rizwan replied that due to the chill and mal-nutrition, the lifestyle of climbing up and down the mountains and related accidents, people out here had various orthopaedic problems. They were too poor to take proper treatment and many lived a handicapped life. He found a lot of fulfilment in serving these people. His dream, life desire and ambitious project were to build a full-fledged hospital in the vicinity and was seeking the Indian Government's support, but it was a long drawn process. He was also looking for help and donations from organizations, apart from the government.

After lunch, people generally settled down on their bunk beds, either chatting with somebody or for an afternoon siesta. Zack leaned against the wall and morosely watched Yamini and Dr. Rizwan chatting and laughing softly at the other end of the room. He was not only feeling lonely and jealous, but he was also not used to being ignored. He had always been the centre of attraction, right from his childhood. He once again started feeling sorry for himself.

He saw people carrying huge bags from the village into the monastery. Some were carrying baskets of vegetables. Some children were lugging a big bag and trying to manoeuvre it up the steps. Zack stood up and went to them. He picked up the bag easily and carried it into the cooking area. There he saw that the contents from the bags the villagers had carried in were being segregated. There was rice, and flour and pulses and vegetables. When a monk saw Zack watching he came over to him and explained that it was the way the villagers were contributing to the feeding of the unexpected guests from the bus- 'them' Zack summarized. 'What generosity and hospitality' he thought. Nobody had to tell or ask. They gave of whatever they had, not worrying about themselves or tomorrow. The monk explained that it was a community living here. Many a time, due to natural calamities, stores are not delivered and transportation stopped. At such times, the villagers take care of each other's needs. It is ensured that everybody is fed and have a roof over their head. Zack thought- one for all and all for one.

He further helped stack the bags on the shelves, especially the higher racks, laughing and joking with the people there. It felt as if all had gathered together for a party, not due to a calamity. Hearing the chatter and laughter, more people came into the room and joined in the conversation. A lad started singing and some others joined him. Zack did not follow the meaning of the lyrics but rhythmically started drumming on a few tins in the kitchen. Immediately many people got up and started dancing. Dr. Rizwan and Yamini were also dancing. Zack also wanted to go and join them, but couldn't stop drumming, else the dancing would stop. After a while, his hands started hurting and he slowed down and gradually was forced to stop. The dancers happily sat down and some went to get a sip of water. Zach went up to Yamini and Dr. Rizwan and sat down beside them and started chatting.

Zack could not hide the tension he was in. Yamini knew what was troubling him. So, she asked him about his family, to divert his mind. Zack started telling her about his family, his childhood. His father had been one of the richest and highly influential men in Austin. He had one elder sister and one younger sister. He had been a pampered, NO, a spoilt brat. But he turned rebel the day he had been packed off to the hostel at the age of 8; a prestigious residential school where only the royalty and the very rich were admitted. His getting an admission there had been another feather in his father's cap. He remembered pleading not to be sent away, then crying and screaming as he left home. After that, he stopped speaking to his father. He never understood why he was forced to go to a hostel when his sisters were allowed to stay and study in the regular school and live in that beautiful house with their parents. He became a recluse. Even during the holidays, he avoided his father like a plague. His mom gifted him a camera for his 11th birthday and that became his love, friend and constant companion. He seemed to have a natural knack for photography, which was much appreciated in his school and his photos regularly featured in the school magazines. He also became the official photographer at school functions. As he grew up, girls flocked to him, not only to create their portfolios but also because he was one of the most handsome, rich and charming boys at school and later at college. His arrogance grew. At his mother's insistence and emotional blackmail, he started speaking to his father, but only formally and when it was unavoidable. 'Sir' replaced 'papa'. The grand finale was on his 23rd birthday. His father handed him the keys to his own cabin in the office, as his birthday gift. He wanted Zack to take over the reins of the business as his junior and start getting trained. Something burst within Zack. Till that day he had not decided what he wanted to do. But on the spur of the moment, he told his dad that he wanted to be a journalist and photographer and had no interest in the family business. There was a big showdown where his father finally shouted that he would disown him. Zack packed his clothes and left home with 420$. There was no looking back. His first few photographs won him a global award and he struck gold. He became popular and world-famous. Within the year he had earned his first million. Within the next year, he had blown it. Soon he earned his next million and blew it. He had lost count of the number of millions he had earned and spent. Today he was back to square one. He had been banking on his interview with the Dalai Lama to pull him through. He had to pay his kids' school fees. Yamini and Dr. Rizwan looked at him, astound. In his whole conversation, he had never mentioned a wife. Zack smiled and said- 'I was married to a perfect doll. I have always had a weakness for petite women [like his mom??]. His wife was a Japanese, whom he had met during a stint at Tokyo. It was love at first sight and marriage at second sight. They had their first child, a daughter within the year. Zack did not want to be away from his family even for a short while. He took up a job at Kodak in Tokyo as a senior consultant. He was earning handsomely. They were in seventh heaven. 3 years later, his wife was pregnant again. This time there were complications and she needed rest and expensive medical treatment. He appointed a cook and also a nanny to take care of his first daughter. There was a house mortgage. Expenses were mounting. He did the only thing that he knew would fetch him a fortune. He picked up his camera and went incognito among the Cambodian rebels for almost 2 months. When he came out, barely alive, and sold the story he became a millionaire many times over. He was a hero. But the bug had gotten into him again. Now there was no holding him to his desk or his home. He started doing more and more adventure stints. Money poured in, but his kids stopped recognizing him. His wife was left to handle the house and 2 small kids, all alone. The gap started widening between them. She became clinging and possessive. She would cry when she saw him and whenever he left, which was at quicker frequency; and nag him whenever he called her. Finally, he stopped calling her and came home after long intervals. He kept transferring money regularly. Once, he decided to surprise her on their wedding anniversary and returned home- and found her partying with his old colleague from kodak. Both were stoned. The kids were playing in their room with the nanny. The nanny looked scared when she saw Zack but finally told him that this was a regular feature. He was risking his life, earning for them, but all the money he sent was spent on partying, drinks and drugs. Bills had not been paid for a long time. Nanny had not been paid for months, but she had stuck on as she loved the kids, having seen them grow from the time they were born.

The next day he went to his lawyer and filed for a divorce. His wife cried and begged for forgiveness. He could have forgiven her, but not the way she had neglected the kids. He won custody of his children, aged 6 and 2. He stayed with them for the next two years with a nanny to take care of them. His wife took a huge slab of his savings along with the divorce and has not bothered to enquire about him or the kids even once in all these years. But money was running out and he had to make some fast decisions. He sent both his children to the same prestigious school where he had studied. Nanny took care of his house in Tokyo where his kids came to, during holidays. He tried to be around them during that time.

Suddenly his eyes filled. He understood how his father must have felt when he had sent Zack to the boarding school.

He shook his head and asked Yamini if she too was going to Dharamsala to meet His Holiness, the Dalai Lama. She shook her head sadly and said-'I wish. But actually, my parents live there. My father had a heart attack 4 days ago. He is admitted in the ICU and my mom is handling everything alone, especially in these raging rains. She is also suffering from arthritis. I was going there to take care of them. I don't know how she is managing. She must be worried stiff about me too now. As it is, she has enough on her plate.' Zack was surprised. She looked so calm, he would never have guessed she was under so much stress. When he said as much, she asked-" how would my ranting or crying change the situation".

she continued-"do you know the famous prayer"-
" Lord, give me the strength to change what I can,
The fortitude to accept what I cannot change,
And the wisdom to know the difference".

Dr. Rizwan elaborated- "most of the times we accept situations as we don't have a choice- like now; or like when you divorced your wife; but many a times we accept situations consciously- like Yamini. She lost her husband to a hit and run case when he was on his morning jog. The police never found the culprit. Her son was 1 year old then. She has been a single parent since then. Now he is a grown-up man- all of 26 years. But she holds no animosity or anger against the killer or life for what it has done to her. She keeps genuinely forgiving everyone and everything and moving ahead. She has seen life in all its facets and has walked away, laughing. Now she knows that she's bigger than any situation life throws at her. That's where her confidence and calmness comes from. That's her beauty. That's why I love her so much". There, he had said it openly. All three of them just smiled.

Zack was surprised at the light and positive atmosphere in the monastery and said as much. Dr. Rizwan explained that it had a lot to do with the monastery. When Zack looked askance, Yamini elaborated-"the architecture of a temple, mosque, church, monastery etc; are constructed in such a way that they draw the energy from the universe into the building and make it divine and positive. So, it is very difficult for people to be depressed or negative here for a long period. Don't we always go to such places when we are disturbed or need solace?"

She continued-" that's the reason you were able to meditate so easily, not once, but twice, today- even though you have never meditated before. That's also the reason why retreats are held in such places, where it's conducive to spirituality. There's so much abundance here". "Abundance" Zack exclaimed. "I only see poverty and suffering here". Dr. Rizwan said slowly, in a measured tone- "usually our inner self is reflected in our vision of the outer world". Zack was shocked and felt insulted. He was in the monastery under dire circumstances, not because he was needy or suffering. He felt his face go red and hot. Yamini took his hand in hers and said- "calm down Zack. You don't understand. Tell me something-

Do you see the abundance of Love here? Is it there in your life?

Do you see the abundance of true Friendship here? Is it there in your life?

Do you see the abundance of Fun and Food here?

Do you see the abundance of Generosity and Good Deeds here?

Do you see the abundance of Energy here?

Do you see the abundance of Spirituality here??

Do you have all this abundance in your life?"

Zack silently shook his head "No", to the questions Yamini was asking-

CHAPTER SIX

The Universe is whispering.........
Show me your New Vibration; I will show you Miracles
~ The Attraction Signal

"There's abundance freely available in this universe for everybody, but it whispers its secrets very softly. That's why not everybody is able to hear it. But sometimes we hear a minuscule whisper accidently and come into abundance. There's so much joy and happiness and wealth in our life at that moment. We are in seventh heaven. But it doesn't last, and we are unable to replicate it because it was accidental and happened without our awareness.

To attract abundance into your life permanently, you have to develop an "Abundance consciousness" within you.

"Abundance consciousness" means- becoming aware that there's plenty of everything, - the Air, the Sun, moon, stars, trees, Rains [laughing]; feeling it from your heart and connecting with it consciously- even if it doesn't seem to be part of your life at this moment, so much so that it becomes part of your subconscious. It's the quality or state of being full, owning everything that's in the universe. It's like.....you see anything and start feeling it's yours.

You cannot be in 'Abundance Consciousness' if you are living a life of incompleteness, restrictions, scantiness, insufficiency, poverty and the like. You cannot be in 'Abundance Consciousness' even if you live a life of anger, jealousy, avarice, greed, miserliness and the like"

Zack sat, listening, but not fully comprehending, glued to her words. She continued-"there is abundance in this world and everyone can be part of it, no matter where, or under what circumstances. But to really partake and enjoy its beauty and richness, one needs to be open to it, expect it, enjoy it, relish it....."

Dr. Rizwan continued- "This conscious awareness then opens your mind and you begin to see it all around you, and more importantly- within you. You begin to recognize opportunities. You begin to break through the limiting beliefs we all carry in our minds. You start feeling you are a part of the abundance of the universe, and you let yourself start thinking in Unlimited ways. You are normally limiting your thoughts to the things that exist in your life right now, but you have to expand your vision and horizons to greater opportunities that exist on this planet and ultimately in the universe". He started laughing at Zack's bemused look.

Zack wonderingly asked how he could become Abundance conscious. Yamini said- "Life is a field bearing unlimited fruits. If you look at what you have in your life, you will always have more and more. If you look at what you lack or don't want in life, you will only have a lack or more of what you don't want. Neither prosperity nor poverty is about having or not having money or wealth. It is a vibration that attracts things, makes you manifest whatever you need or want. It is a way of living and thinking".

She continued- "I put my son through one of the costliest colleges in the country. His annual fees was more than my annual salary at that time. But I was confident of manifesting the required money for his fees. And it happened. He graduated from the best college. That was my commitment to him, like how you are committed to giving the best facilities to your kids".

Let me share a funny incident with you, she said. - "I have always been very fond of cars, but at a particular phase in life, I couldn't afford to buy one. My dream was to have a dark blue Zen car, which was the latest car in the market then. One day I went to one of my family friend's house and there was a big argument going on there. Their son was leaving for New York for six months and his father was after him to sell his car, as his friends would constantly come to borrow it, in their son's absence. Their son didn't want to sell it.

When I landed there, they made me the arbitrator. Suddenly their son looked at me and said- 'Didi, you keep the car at your place and use it till I return. My friends will not even know where it is.' His parents were also very happy with this solution and the car landed up at my place. A few days later, I was admiring the car from my balcony and suddenly realized – it was a dark blue Zen!! Their son stayed in New York for over 2 years and I had the car to myself.

I used to keep doodling drawings of the house I dreamt of building. Finally, when I purchased my flat, can you believe it, it turned out to be the same design as my drawings, even the dimensions of the rooms were the same.

Oh my God. So many incidents. I could go on and on".

"Is it all it takes- think of something, for it to manifest?"- Zach asked unbelievingly.

"No, no" Yamini smiled. "There's a secret method to this thinking too. I will tell you about it some other time - when the time is right".

CHAPTER SEVEN

Struggle ends where Gratitude begins
~ Neale D Walsh

She asked for a book and pencil from one of the monk lads, which he got for her within a few minutes. She smiled at me and said – "you have home work to do now, Zack!! First you have to recognize all the blessings you have. Once you do that, the lack will take care of itself. Start writing all that you have, starting from your breath and your handsome body.......when you are done, we will discuss further" She said, handing me the book and pencil, and walked away jauntily.

Zack picked up the pencil and started chewing on it. He bit into the dirty bitter eraser at the end of it and disgustedly spat it out. Yamini had easily told him to write his blessings. He couldn't think of a single thing.

Be grateful for his breathing? What was the use of him breathing now. It was past 3 PM and his appointment with His Holiness, the Dalai Lama was at 4.30PM. There was no way he could reach Dharamsala within the hour. His contract was gone. He was bankrupt. His father was correct. He should have taken over his father's trading business. At least there was plenty of money in it. But he could never visualize himself behind a huge desk in an AC room, all suited and booted. Both, his grandfather and father had been into trading and were one of the richest and most influential families in Austin. He had always been adventurous, right from childhood. Even the hellish heat of Texas could not stop him from spending all his free time outdoors. He had been fairly good at academics, but had excelled at all sports. He had filled the house with medals and trophies. His father had got special shelves made just to showcase his trophies, that too in the living room and it was the first thing his mother would speak about to their guests. How proud they had been of his achievements!

He had walked out of his house and inheritance the day he had told his father that he wanted to be a photographer and journalist and not a stock broker. But he had done very well for himself. When his very first set of photographs had won the prize in a global contest, he had been an instant success. He had not only become an instant millionaire, but also one of the most popular photographers around the world. He had made his father proud of him all over again, but not happy. Even on his deathbed, his father has reminded him that photography could only be a hobby and not a career. But what pierced Zack's heart that day was not dad's words, but the tears in dad's eyes. Fortunately both his sisters had taken over the reins of the business, else he might have just worn the tie and sat behind the desk, out of guilt. He had been lucky there too.

His mother's face, full of love and pride flashed before his eyes. He had such a wonderful, loving family. He had not even spoken to them since Christmas, and that too had been a short call to wish them Merry Christmas. He had been so busy drowning in his own life.

He picked up the book and pencil and wrote his first blessing-

A loving mother and 2 sisters, their husbands and 3 beautiful nieces. He decided that he would go to visit them with his children, first thing as soon as he left India.

Two wonderful, beautiful children who loved him the most on earth.

A career which he loved and enjoyed. Very few people were as lucky as him to enjoy their profession and also earn fame and fortune.

A healthy mind and body which allowed him to enjoy his profession and life.

All the varied experiences and adventures he had enjoyed.

His first trophy in running race at the age of 6; his photo on the national sports magazine when he had captioned the football team and won the world cup. His father had thrown a huge party in his honour. So much joy and happiness in his life, which he had not recognized all this time.

He kept remembering every instance in his life and writing his blessings. The list seemed endless. At some point he felt so grateful for all the goodness in his life, tears of gratitude started flowing freely down his face. He realized it when his tears dropped down on the page on which he was writing. He felt too choked with emotion. He could no longer continue writing. He put his pencil down. He was totally exhausted and also felt curiously light, as if, along with the pencil he had laid down a huge burden he had been carrying on his shoulders. He curled down on the floor and went into a deep sleep.

CHAPTER EIGHT

Nothing brings down walls, as surely as Acceptance
~ Deepak Chopra

He wasn't aware of how long he had slept, but he suddenly woke up to shouting and wailing. He looked at his watch and realized that he had dozed off for barely 15 minutes. But he was feeling totally refreshed. He picked up his precious camera and rushed out and stood shell shocked. The rains had stopped. But the water was gushing with great force from the mountains, straight towards them. There was no way they could escape the flood. Even as they watched in horror, huge chunks of the mountain started sliding down in slow motion. The whole mountain was collapsing. Then boulders started rolling down, at first slowly than with increasing velocity. It was as if they were competing with each other to win the Olympics. People started chanting their last prayers. Zack's only sorrow was that he would die without meeting his mom. He prayed to God that he should be given another chance to be a better son to her, if not this birth, at least in the next. He had never believed in births and reincarnations, but he must be becoming fatalistic due to the company he was with.

The boulders kept thundering down but suddenly some of them changed direction and veered into the valley below. Miracle of miracles, the boulders had impeded the speed of the water. It was flowing down with much less ferocity, but still dangerously. The boulders had also changed the direction of the water a little bit. Much less water was now flowing into the village, though even that was enough to flood many houses. Houses started falling like cardboard boxes. The villagers started screaming and crying, seeing their possessions and animals being washed away by the torrent. The water gushed into the foyer of the monastery and rushed into the ground floor rooms. Everybody ran towards the monastery as if their life depended on it, which it did, of course. The water was steadily rising. Everybody started rushing up the narrow stairs to the open terrace of the monastery, this being the only strong building in the whole area, strong enough to withstand the flood, Hopefully!! Zack had reflexively started filming the horror and destruction being caused by the flooding waters from the start, without even realizing it.

He now really understood the true meaning of gratitude and thanksgiving. He did not need a book to write it down. Gratitude was now overflowing in his Mind and his heart. He thanked God for this second chance at life from the bottom of his heart. But now what?? The water had now flooded into the ground floor of the monastery. The possibility was that his backpack would have also floated away in the floodwaters, along with everybody else's. His last currency- $ 1670 and Rs.2340/-was also gone. His passport and Visa were gone. His clothes are gone. He was literally on the streets. He might as well die. His kids would at least get his substantial insurance amount, which would take care of their education. They had the house and he was sure their nanny would take care of them, come what may.

Oh My God!! He sat down on the wet floor of the terrace, head in his hands, totally dejected. His family would not even know if he was alive or dead as he had the habit of disappearing for long months on end. He felt a hand on his shoulder and thought it was his Angel- Yamini. But it was Dr. Rizwan. Dr.Rizwan sat down next to him and said "I know how you are feeling. But we all have to accept that this is the reality now".

Zack asked angrily-" so how does my accepting or not accepting a situation make any difference?"

Dr. Rizwan said-" SO, shall we start from your childhood. Just imagine, if instead of revolting, you had accepted that your parents were sending you to the best of boarding school for your own good. You would not only have enjoyed your school days but also not mess up the relationship with your father, right".

"NOW, how does accepting that fact make a difference"- Zack was getting irritated by this flashback talk.

"I know it's very difficult for you to accept that you were responsible for everything that happened in your life, every single thing. But you are not interested in accepting that because it will also make you responsible for the situation you are in today. As a kid you could not run away from school or your father. But since then, you have been running away from every situation life has given you. That's why it was so easy for you to roam the forests and mountains, living with animals and militants. There was no question of acceptance there".

"But I was happily married for 6 years, wasn't I ?" Zack growled angrily. How could Dr. Rizwan say he was responsible for all his mess. "This time you are wrong Dr. Rizwan. It was my wife Annette who messed up our marriage. You can't blame me for it" Zack gave a sad smile.

"Actually I can" Dr. Rizwan said softly. Zack's head jerked up. Dr. Rizwan continued-"did you not say your wife was a doll, petite and clingy. She loved someone taking care of her, right. In fact that's what attracted you to her". Zack nodded. "Then was it right on your part to leave her to manage everything all alone, that too with two small kids, for months on end, not even knowing if you were alive or dead?!"

"But I was doing it for her, the kids. She was living royally, only because I was taking those risks".

"Were both of you not happy when you were working with kodak, Zack? Could you have not got another job at kodak or a similar one? You went once due to circumstances, but was it necessary for you to keep going - after that? You knew your wife was upset and angry with you for what you were doing. Do you think only you have the right to be angry and to rebel, only you have the right to give up your family business and take up the camera and roam around, but your wife should not get angry or rebel, right? Is that fair? Are you not responsible for her condition? In fact, I would say you ruined her life for your own selfish ends, not the other way round".

Zack felt he had been punched really hard in his solar plexus. He understood how he had been running away all his life and blaming others for his condition. Even now his children must be worrying their heads off about him. And he always thought he was doing them a favour by spending their holidays with them. As a parent he knew he wanted the best for his children, yet he had punished his parents for wanting the best for him. Oh God. Will they ever forgive him? Could he ever forgive himself?

It was as if Dr. Rizwan had read his mind. "now.... don't go blaming and cursing yourself for all that happened. Everybody makes mistakes, especially in their younger years. It's out of ignorance, which is forgivable. But its unforgivable if you continue with the act even after realizing the truth".

Zack nodded and looked at Dr. Rizwan gratefully. Then suddenly he turned and hugged him tight. He surprised himself. He had never been the demonstrative type. Even with Annette, he always felt she should understand his love because he was doing so much for her. Even risking dangers to keep her in style. He guessed he was like his father. The thought brought a happy smile. Until yesterday, such a thought would have had him boiling. Today, it made him feel happy to realize that he had his father's characteristic in him. His father could also never share his thoughts or emotions. Perhaps if he had, things would have been different. There he went, blaming others for his weaknesses. But his mother had also led a lonely life. But she had dedicated her life to her 3 children and charities, never complaining.

When he mentioned this, Dr. Rizwan said "different people react differently to situations. It also depends on their upbringing and the values they have been inculcated with. You have been brought up with strong values, so you are able to immediately understand what Yamini and I are saying, and relate it to your life. But another person might not be, or might not care to! Believe me, not everybody wants to get out of their comfort zone, or come down to earth from the pedestal they have placed themselves on. It's very, very difficult to turn yourself inside out. I am impressed and admire you for it. All of us are lonely in some way or the other. How we handle it is in our hands. But! now comes the big question. Are you going to do something about all this realization, and if so, what? Think deeply about it".

Zack already knew what he had to do. First and foremost, he would make peace with his mom, sisters and family. They were his greatest assets. With them around he had everything. Without them, he would be poor even if he had all the wealth in the world. His children also deserved to know about the wonderful grandparent and relatives they had. How happy they would be. And how happy his mother would be, to meet his children. Zack had a big smile on his face.

The smile slowly faded. He would go find Anette. Not to get back with her. It was over. But he definitely wanted to know if she was ok. He would be there for her if she needed any help. Just thinking about these decisions made him feel so much better, so good, so complete.

He never realized till now that it had started raining steadily. There was no food tonight, no shelter, no warm clothes. He never realized how lucky he had been yesterday, to get these things. He had only been bothered about his interview with His Holiness, the Dalai Lama, his contract, the fortune he would have got for it.

Everybody sat in the dark – hungry, thirsty, shivering in the cold, silent with their own thoughts. Even the children were quiet. Even they did not ask for food or water. But they were all of them praying, not out of fear or desperation, but chanting calmly, just waiting, knowing that they are somehow being taken care of. There was an eerie silence. And Zack also sat there, shivering away, feeling curiously calm. The chanting was very rhythmic and soothing. It did not disturb him that Yamini and Dr. Rizwan were not to be seen anywhere. He was not troubled by the situation outside or inside him. There must be some purpose to what was happening. He felt, whatever happened, it was okay. He just had to wait and watch. At that moment he realized how much power there was in ACCEPTANCE.

CHAPTER NINE

Generosity is a practical expression of Love
~ Gary Inrig

Around the early hours of the morning, maybe 3.30 AM, it just stopped raining. A gentle breeze started blowing, making it even colder, but curiously soothing. Everybody actually started taking deep breaths and sighs could be heard. Some people, including Zack, got up and stretched themselves. Zach switched on his camera and started filming all the people on the terrace, just to bring cheer. A huge grin appeared on their faces, especially the children- who started posing. There was general laughter and chatter. The atmosphere grew more cheerful- less desperate. Dawn started painting orange streaks in the canvas of the sky and the rising sun appeared on the horizon. The chatter on the terrace grew louder. Children started complaining that they were hungry. Through all the noise, a curious whirring sound was heard in the skies. Immediately everybody became silent. Everybody's eyes turned towards the sound. Two helicopters were making their way towards the terrace. Immediately some men and the senior monks started organizing the people gathered on the terrace. All the people were herded to one side of the huge terrace and space made for the helicopters to land. There was sufficient space for one helicopter to land. Zack continued to silently film the whole procedure. One helicopter landed and huge bags were brought out from it. Two men carried them to where the people were huddled and handed sandwich packets and a bottle of water to each and every one. Everybody immediately opened the packets and started gobbling the food hungrily. Then 6 of the oldest and the lady with the infant were herded into the helicopter which took off to the monastery in Dharamsala, where arrangements had been made for everybody's stay. Within a few minutes, the second helicopter which was hovering above landed and the next batch was flown off. Zack started searching desperately for Dr. Rizwan and Yamini, asking everybody about their whereabouts, but nobody seemed to know anything. Finally, the helicopter pilot who overheard his enquiries told him that they were safe in Dharamsala. Zack couldn't believe it. How could those two leave everybody to their fate last night and fly off to safety first? The pilot continued to explain that they had braved the lashing rains and floodwaters to reach Dr. Rizwan's half-drowned hospital, where he had a wireless radio, and had contacted help for everybody here. Since they had been in deep waters, literally, they had been rescued first and flown to safety.

Zack had heard the quote 'Faith moves mountains but had never grasped the full meaning of it till now. Within 4 hours, everybody from the terrace had been flown to the monastery in Dharamshala. Everybody was given a bed, fresh robes, piping hot Thupka to fill their stomach and later, a sealed packet. When Zack opened the envelope, he found Rs.50,000/- in it. It had been given by the government to the flood victims, to compensate them for their losses and see them through their immediate expenses. Zack couldn't believe it. This amount would take care of his needs for at least a month, including buying a few clothes for him, if he handled it carefully. Everybody was in a better mood now, first, being saved from the crises and now having some money in their hands. The government had also promised some more money for reconstructing their houses once the floods subsided, concrete houses- stronger than before.

Zach got to know that His Holiness, the Dalai Lama was in the monastery and ran around literally half-clothed, immediately setting the wheels rolling for an interview with his holiness, but was politely refused. The Dalai Lama was leaving the monastery shortly to fly abroad. "But his holiness had a message for Zack. He told Zack to hold all that he had learnt now- close to his heart. Happiness would always be his" Zack was not satisfied with any special messages and was becoming desperate; just within hands reach and yet so far!! He could not think of what to do.

He walked despondently to his room. He found that his mobile, which he had plugged in for charging before going in search of His Holiness was now fully charged. Thankfully, he called his friend, Rajesh Sinha, in Delhi, who was also a fellow journalist in a leading Indian TV channel. Rajesh was over-joyed to hear Zack's voice and to know that he was safe, and that too with his holiness, the Dalai Lama. He had been desperately worried, knowing that Zack would have been caught up in the heavy downpour and the consequent floods.

Zack explained all that had happened with him in the past 3 days; - just 3 days!! Oh My God. It seemed like a lifetime. Suddenly Rajesh started shouting with joy. Zack couldn't understand what was making his friend so happy, especially when he was not getting his coveted interview with the Dalai Lama. Rajesh was over-joyed that Zack had filmed all the happenings of the past few days and had first-hand records of the whole crisis, including the rescue. He offered to buy all of them, first rights, for his TV channel. And the price he quoted for it made Zack stagger. He could not believe his ears. It was much more than he had been expecting to make from his interview with the Dalai Lama. Tears started flowing freely down his face. But this time they were tears of joy and gratefulness. He promised to return to Delhi at the earliest possible and hand over the videos to Rajesh.

He then called his children and promised them that he would return home in a weeks' time. He called his mom. He did not know what he would say as he was speaking to her after so long. Even his Christmas calls had fizzled to cards and later texts. He felt ashamed of himself. His younger sister picked up the call and could not believe her ears. She ran shouting through the house, calling out to everybody. Zack could not believe that they were not angry with him, but over-joyed to hear from him. His mom was too choked to even speak to him for a few moments. They were all waiting for Zack to come to his senses and return home. Zack did not know what to say. He promised his mom that he would visit her very soon with his children. He felt so happy when he said that. His family would be complete once more. Just the thought made his heart expand till he thought it would burst with joy. His gratitude knew no bounds. He kept repeatedly thanking God, without even realizing that he was doing so.

Then his elder sister took over the phone and told him that they had been desperately searching for him for the past few days. She said there was a surprise awaiting him. She refused to say anything more about it. Even during their childhood days, she would always speak in riddles and plan surprises for everybody. Zack did not give it another thought. After speaking to his family for some more time,

Zack knew what he had to do. God had been too kind to him, too many times. It was now time for him to repay.

He went in search of Dr. Rizwan and Yamini. He found them in the gardens, after quite a search. When they saw him in the monastery robe, barely reaching his knees and not even covering his chest, both burst into uncontrollable laughter. Zack joined in self-consciously. After a hearty laugh, they caught up with each other's news. Zack proudly told them all that had taken place with him and how he had patched up with his family. Yamini, the all-knowing, told him that she had known things would work out for him. When he gave her a disbelieving look, she said-"Zack, you were born into abundance; it's in your DNA. You may be broke, but you will never be poor. It's like the river finding its way to the ocean. The river may dry up occasionally but ultimately will flow to fill the ocean".

Zack did not understand all this talk of DNA but knew he wanted to empty some of his ocean. He hugged Dr. Rizwan and told him that he would donate a substantial amount for building Dr. Rizwan's dream hospital in the mountains, from the money he was getting from Rajesh. For a change, Zach saw tears forming in Dr. Rizwan and Yamini's eyes, instead of his own.

He joking called their group- "the weepers", to which Yamini replied-" there's an old saying- "A young man who has never cried is a savage, and an old man who has never laughed is a fool".

Zack broodingly said –" I have learnt so much from you in the past 2 days. My life has changed. I don't want to leave your company".

Yamini replied-"what you have learnt is just a scratch on the surface, so superficial. If that has made such a deep impact on you, just imagine how much more powerful my whole course is. I coach people to lead Abundant lives. I also conduct programs on how to transform their lives and become powerful Leaders, in every aspect of life. Zack, if you are interested, you can also learn all the secrets and lead a Complete, Happy, Prosperous and Fulfilling life. It just takes 10 weeks and your 100% commitment".

Zack laughed –" I don't know if I can ever dedicate 10 full weeks continuously, in my lifetime. You know I have so many loose ends to tie up, so much to do. And... I don't even know where you live or have your phone number".

Yamini said-" I have left my phone in the room, to dry, after it got soaked in the rains yesterday. Hope it's still in working condition. But you can note down my number. The world is so small now, Zack. We can reach anyone- across the world. My courses are also conducted via zoom to any corner of the Globe. And it's not for hours on end for 10 weeks. It's only for 1-2 hours, one day a week, for 10 weeks".

Zack was so happy to hear the details that he promised to commence the course from the following week itself, where ever he was. He hugged both of them and bid goodbye, as he wanted to shop for some clothes and leave for Delhi at the earliest.

In the final round, the helicopters had rescued some of the luggage they had found. Zach's backpack, which he had secured to the bunk-bed post had also been rescued. He thanked his stars for his habit of always securely packing his clothes in waterproof vacuum bags- to save space and keep them wrinkle-free. His stints in the dense forests and mountains had taught him many such life lessons, which always stood him in good stead. Now he did not have to waste time buying clothes, either. He could leave for Delhi at the earliest. He jumped eagerly into his own fresh clothes and checked to see if his passport and other papers were safe.

With a heart bursting with joy and gratitude, Zack climbed into the Volvo bus that night, on his return journey to Delhi. He had come here chasing a rainbow; he was returning with the pot of gold at the end of the Rainbow.

COMMANDMENTS

- BE BRAVE AND COURAGEOUS. Always remember- you are much bigger than every situation life throws at you.
- MEDITATE regularly. It clears the mind and relieves stress, apart from numerous other benefits.
- BE GRATEFUL always. Maintain a journal of all your blessings and always be aware of how blessed and lucky you are.
- LAUGHTER. Always find a reason to laugh. It may not add Years to your Life, but it will definitely add Life to your Years.
- ACCEPT the inevitable. "People often make 2 mistakes in their quest for inner peace-
- Focusing on things they cannot change – and Ignoring things they can change" [Anonymous]
- BE GENEROUS. Always share your blessings for the benefit of the less fortunate.
- These are but very, very few superficial tips. There are many more deep and deeper secrets to Abundance which the universe keeps whispering. Pay attention and listen carefully and keep learning them, whenever the Universe offers you the opportunity.
- Everybody interested in undertaking this journey of Abundance and Transformational Leadership further in their life can contact **Chitra** -
- paradigmsoar@gmail.com / www.paradigmsoar.com

www.ingramcontent.com/pod-product-compliance
Lightning Source LLC
LaVergne TN
LVHW041545060526
838200LV00037B/1139